HOW TO
POO
IN THE WOODS

Published in 2015 by Prion
an imprint of the Carlton Publishing Group
20 Mortimer Street
London W1T 3JW

Text copyright © 2015 Mats and Enzo
Design copyright © 2015 Carlton Books Limited

Original illustration artworks: Williams Design Studio
All other photographs and illustrations supplied by iStock.com & Shutterstock.com

ISBN 978-1-85375-934-5

A catalogue record of this book can be obtained from the British Library

Printed in China

1 3 5 7 9 10 8 6 4 2

HOW TO
POO
IN THE WOODS

Mats & Enzo

PRION

CONTENTS

When we first talked about writing a book on pooing in the woods, reactions were very strong. Many mocked the new subject matter, telling us it was too simple, and certainly not one that required a manual. The main argument was that humans have been shitting in the woods for millennia – ever since we were humans and, indeed, before that; it was something natural and certainly didn't require instructions. We were asked – often with venom – why we didn't instead write a manual about *How to Breathe*, *How to Lift up Your Arms* or *How to Grow Nose Hair*.

Of course, it was precisely because of these reactions, putting us in the eye of the (shit) storm, that we knew we had picked the right subject and had a future bestseller on our hands. We were in the same situation when working on *How to Poo at Work*, the now legendary book that has changed and continues to change office culture in companies everywhere. Things are quite simple in the world of book publishing: when a subject provokes such virulent reaction, it proves it is touching our most hidden, common fears and is hitting the mark.

Our minds were made up. We were going to tackle this new taboo subject: pooing in the woods. We would turn this issue upside down and take no shit for it. We were ready once more to face the consequences. We decided to shake up the *omerta* that has kept it taboo, even though it is common in all sectors of human outdoor activity – walkers, hunters, anglers, horseback riders, cross-country skiers, ornithologists and all other -ists who go into the woods, as well as many other communities and tribes who run around forests sneakily relieving themselves without admitting it, not even to their closest friends. We were not going to lose sight of the forest for the trees, because we knew that everyone has or will poo in the woods at one time or another. We have even found proof of this in the field. We know the techniques, and the time has come for us to reveal them. This takes courage, like the courage needed by Bob Woodward and Carl Bernstein in 1972. We, Mats & Enzo, are here – the modern-day Bob and Carl – not afraid to flee from the challenge.

The tragic loss of ancestral techniques

We humans are at our best when exchanging new information and ideas. A person thinking alone in a corner won't accomplish much. Humanity made its biggest advances through the meetings of the minds; through an exchange, a debate and confrontation of ideas. Libraries played an enormous role in this, gathering all the knowledge acquired thus far. They ensured that the conversation of great minds such as Thales, Aristotle, Socrates, Copernicus, Newton continued from one century to another. Great cities, such as Rome or New York, became melting pots of different peoples and traditions, which also facilitated the exchange of ideas and knowledge.

It was thanks to all of this that we have advanced enough to be able to watch funny cat videos from the other side of the planet without leaving our houses. Today, we can see six funny cats per minute in a YouTube video, or 360 funny cats per hour. Scientists calculated that an ancient Egyptian wanting to see the same number of funny cats would have had to observe Egyptian cats for nine hours per day for six years and three months.

In the great flow of knowledge and constant advances in human development, however, there is one subject that got stuck in the same spot: pooing in the woods. We always used to exchange information and make new discoveries in this field, but it has now been several centuries since this stopped. Before that it wasn't uncommon to happen upon such conversations on this topic:

"Ah, you do it that way. Look, this is how I do it."

"Bend forward just a little bit more, you'll be more stable, you'll see."

"No! Don't ever wipe yourself with that leaf! I did it yesterday and haven't been able to walk since!"

"You could also use roses to eliminate the odour."

"Remember I was in Norway last summer? Do you want to know how the Vikings poop in the woods? They go in groups of 100, and all of them scream and bang their swords on their shields in unison."

"You see, this is Stonehenge*. It is unique in the world – a big circle marking the spot where all travellers must poo. It's a new thing. It's quite clever because this protects the water sources from being soiled."

This is how hundreds of millions of tips on the best ways to poo in the woods were passed down from one person to another, from one century to the next, from one continent to another. Thanks to this, humanity kept advancing and bettering itself.

But not so long ago, this transfer of knowledge ceased. Historians estimate that this can be traced to the end of the Middle Ages, when relieving oneself in the woods began to be seen as shameful. At that time people started inventing excuses to slip away for a few minutes in order to alleviate their intense intestinal pressure.

This new attitude established itself over several centuries and didn't touch all social classes at the same time. At first it was the aristocracy in the south of England who began to hide when pooing in the woods. While fox hunting, it became common to hear one participant telling the other that he just needs to step away for a minute to check if that wasn't a fox or a wild boar that he saw with a corner of the eye. Inevitably, he came back saying that no, it was just leaves or a big snail. Soon, in the refined circles of English fox hunters, the expression "I think I saw a fox" became a polite way of saying: "I have an urgent need to poo to attend to; please don't look for me for the next five minutes."

The shameful notion of pooing in the woods and of going to the toilet in general then quickly established itself in the bourgeoisie. It only took a few decades for new expressions to appear in the middle classes, such as: "I have to powder my nose." The working class followed suit. (It was also in this time, coincidentally, that constipation, thus far an non-existent problem, appeared. Diarrhoea, however, has always existed.)

All of this wouldn't be such a tragedy if it hadn't been accompanied by a continual loss of knowledge about the best techniques of pooing in

8

the woods. It was easy for the first aristocrats who began to pretend they never relieved themselves, since they still knew all the techniques that their ancestors had passed on to them without shame. Increasingly, however, this knowledge of the best techniques was forgotten until it all but disappeared. Everyone was soon left to their own devices when faced with the need to poo in the woods. As a result, our current knowledge of this subject today is inferior to that of the Neanderthal.

This is why it is of the utmost importance that we overcome our now established social mores and gather what is left of our knowledge of the best techniques in this area. We hope that this book will be the first building block upon which we can begin to make new advances in how to poo in the woods. We dream of a world in which Facebook pages will be created to exchange photos and tips on the best techniques of outdoor pooing, a world where debate on this topic will be reignited across continents on social media, in all languages. We dream of a world where the hashtag "PooInWoods" will take over Twitter and facilitate the exchange of techniques, feedback, anecdotes and advice; a world where action photos of pooing in the woods with lovely filters will flood Instagram; a world where the *Guardian* will finally publish its first article on the subject and where scientific journals will stop rejecting submissions about it.

The loss of all the knowledge of outdoor poo techniques is a tragedy for humanity. But we are sure that by coming together, we can reinvent lost techniques in two or three centuries at most. We want to be with you at the forefront of the relaunch of this formidable exchange.

This book also aims to look at the ecological aspects of pooing in the woods. In our pages labelled Save the Planet you will discover how to relieve yourself in the forest without harming the environment. We will also share with you the advice from the best natural parks around the world, as well as the crucial importance of a poo trowel and a poo tube in saving our environment.

* According to experts, Stonehenge was the world's first 'motorway' service station toilets.

Take pleasure in pooing in the woods

What we are trying to do with this book is twofold. Firstly, we want to teach you all the techniques you need in order to relieve yourself in the woods. Secondly – and this can come only after you master all the techniques – we want you to enjoy it! Follow our advice, and we guarantee that you will soon be looking forward to your outdoor poos as much as you do to the breathtaking views from mountaintops.

We won't lie: it won't be easy. If you don't live near a forest, you will have to allocate two to three hours a day for outdoor poo training in your garden or your park. If you ever have five minutes to spare, don't waste them: do squats and other exercises that will train your outdoor pooing muscles.

It will be worth your while, we promise. There are poo spots high in the mountains with views that will take your breath away. Satisfying and memorable poos are to be had in magnificent, untouched forests. Stepping away from your group of fellow hikers will also give you the opportunity for close encounters with the wildlife. (Hopefully of the non-violent kind.) You may be encouraged to learn that some participants of the Poo in the Woods workshops led by us in the past have gone on to start blogs about pooing in the woods or to start their own outdoor poo workshops when previously they could not even leave their homes for fear of the dangers of an outdoor poo. How about that for progress! This book will be your welcome travel companion in the years to come. Our biggest reward will be to see an Instagram photo of you, smiling and relaxed, pooing in a part of the forest where other hikers would never dare to relieve themselves.

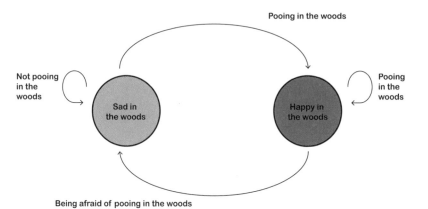

The virtuous circle of pooing in the woods

The expert

We did not need to look far for the expert to guide us on our journey. We have asked Tom Hayatt to join us again and to grace our book with his advice. Those of you familiar with our writing will know that Tom was essential in the making of our first book, *How to Poo at Work*. He is without question the world's Number Two expert in workplace toilets (there is no Number One). His demanding work, where there is no room for error, is incredibly stressful, which is why he often relaxes outdoors. But before we touch upon this aspect of his life, let's review his incredible professional journey.

Tom Hayatt quickly became an indisputable authority on the subject of toilets in the workplace. It was he who first shed light on the issue in the prestigious *Management Journal of the Massachusetts Institute of Technology* in a 1987 article, "Real Social Working Dynamics for Water Closets". At first he was not taken seriously presumably because the subject was considered frivolous, but in 1992 he was finally recognized by his peers, who awarde him the Golden Toilet Brush. His name was also circulated as a possible candidate for a Nobel Prize in Economics. He is often associated with the acronym TML3S, a mnemonic tool used by several executives to remember the dangers that lurk on the way to the toilets and avoid any faux pas. TML3S stands for "Trace, Movement, Light, Shadow, Sound, Smell". Today, Tom Hayatt has circled the globe to speak at conferences.

Tom has spent a total of 16 years in the woods, often by himself. As a highly motivated professional he can never disconnect from his work. Right from the very beginning of his forest adventures, he asked himself questions: How can we poo in the woods in the most efficient manner? What are the techniques that other hikers use in secret? Could my TML3S technique be applied to pooing in the forest? Could I publish articles on this subject in the biggest scientific journals?

This led Tom to undetake new research: he started to look for innovative solutions and techniques for pooing in the woods. He undertook experiments.

He scoured libraries for ancient techniques from across the world. He found nothing. Last year he went to live among pygmies, to study their habits. He wanted to find out if their shorter size, and the fact that their colon is closer to the ground, led them to develop methods that differ from our own. (It didn't.)

We were very impressed by Tom Hayatt's Poo Log. Since the very beginning, he has meticulously noted down the details of each of his poos in the woods in dozens of little notebooks. His notes contain important details: time, wiping method, the incline of the terrain, wind speed, density of hikers per km^2, satellite imagery, etc. All this information was compiled in databases in order to create analyses and cross-analyses to establish the most important trends. A great portion of advice in this book comes from this data: Tom wanted to make all these statistics available to the public as soon as possible. At the end of this book, Tom Hayatt will show you how to build a magnificent toilet out of wood logs for less than £5.

Warning – No Poo in the Woods Syndrome

At the beginning of the hike	15 days later

Sadly, there are people who just cannot relieve themselves away from their home, suffering from what some call the shy bowel syndrome. We have identified a variation of it, No Poo in the Woods Syndrome, for those who only have this problem outdoors. Such people often just can't resist the call of the great outdoors (but sadly can resist the call of nature) and so they venture onto the trails crossing the Alps, the Pyrenees, British forests or Russian taiga. With each passsing day, their suffering increases.

The problem is that hikers suffering from No Poo in the Woods Syndrome are too shy to mention their condition to their guide or fellow hikers. They keep the problem to themselves because they think it's something to be ashamed of.

Fortunately, it's quite easy to spot the signs of this syndrome in your friends. Check the pictures you took of your friend at the beginning of the trip with those from a few days later. A silhouette that seems to have enlarged with time around the belly makes it absolutely certain that your friend is suffering from the No Poo in the Woods Syndrome. In this case you must act quickly. Call the emergency services to come and winch your friend up in a helicopter for immediate evacuation to the nearest hospital, where professionals can pump out the contents of the afflicted intestines.

However, note that the majority of people who suffer from No Poo in the Woods Syndrome will adamantly refuse to be helped. Try saying to your friend: "Paul, I have an impression that you have problems pooping. I haven't seen you go since the beginning of our trip, have I?" In 95% of cases, your friend will deny it. It's understandable! He certainly wouldn't want the guide to bring together the whole group and announce, "Guys, I have bad news. Paul will be ending our hike here because he hasn't been able to poop since the beginning of our trip."

The afflicted certainly don't want looks of pity or advice from other hikers – or worse, offers to accompany them in groups of two or three to help them find out what's the matter. They know that as soon as everyone one is back home there will be stories like this doing the rounds: "We had a bloke on our trip who couldn't shit the whole time, and he almost doubled in size because of it! He had to be evacuated in a helicopter. I'm not kidding you, true story!"

Air-lifting a hiker suffering from No Poo in the Woods Syndrome.

And there's bound to be someone posting kind messages like this on Facebook: "Hey, Paul, hope your colon cleanse went well and that you can poop again!"

That is why you should help your friend by pretending that you need the helicopter for yourself, for whatever reason you think of. Once the rescue team will arrive, they will quickly see who needs help and why, and air-lift your friend to hospital, where he can be properly treated.

BASIC SKILLS

Our techniques will make it possible for you to relieve yourself anywhere in nature, whatever the surrounding vegetation or terrain. You will soon be able to face any situation. So please don't write to our publishers or create Facebook groups asking for a follow-up to this book entitled *How to Poo in the Woods When There Are No Woods*. Read the techniques we suggest for your forest forays, then observe your environment and adapt these techniques to the situation. Once you have read this book, you will be able to poo anywhere in nature, we guarantee it. Trust yourself and your natural capacities!

NO MATTER HOW FAR YOU GO FROM THE TRAIL AND HOW CAREFULLY YOU PICK YOUR SPOT, SOMEONE WILL WALK RIGHT BY YOU THE MOMENT YOU POO.

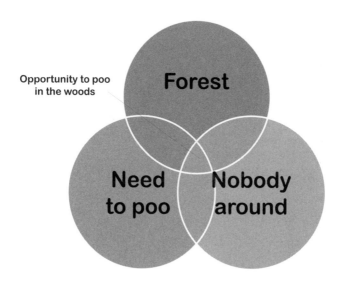

Opportunity to poo
in the woods

Forest

**Need
to poo**

**Nobody
around**

Typical path of a hiker wanting to poo in the woods

When looking for the perfect spot to poo, hikers tend to be very indecisive. Here is a typical path a hiker will take to find an area where they would like to relieve themselves.

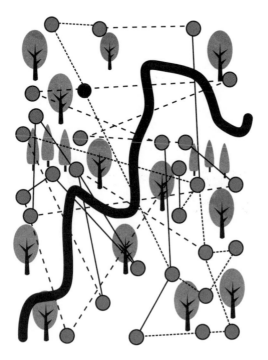

Key:

⬤ A spot taken into consideration but then abandoned.

● The chosen spot.

—————— Walking normally.

- - - - - - - Walking while clenching one's buttocks.

··············· Running in panic, furiously clenching one's buttocks.

When in a new forest or national park, always ask the locals for advice

When you come to a new forest, a new environment or a new country, we strongly advise you to ask the first people you come across for advice. Ask them what the rules are for pooping in the woods in this area, whether there are dedicated poo zones and what fines you can expect for different infractions and quantities.

If you see a sign you don't understand, find a forest ranger and ask for an explanation. If you ask a ranger who doesn't speak English, mime what you need to, in order to avoid problems with local authorities. If necessary, ask this question by miming too. Perform the situation you are asking about by gesticulating and using onomatopoeic sounds (prffffftttttt, plop, plop,...), then hold your nose. Ask if this practice is allowed in his park by pointing to the sky, then look in the ranger's eyes and wait for the doubtless very interesting answer to your question.

DIG→POOP→WIPE

Once you find a safe spot in the forest to relieve yourself, dig a hole with a small shovel or trowel. The hole should be big enough for the poo not to go over the edges. With experience, you will know what your ideal size hole is. From an environmental standpoint, your hole should be as deep as possible.

Position yourself over it, relax, and do your deed peacefully.

Close up the hole, put away your trowel, and leave slowly, perhaps whistling, as if you were just having a bit of a walk around the forest.

IMPORTANT: Hikers using the trowel technique must think ahead and not wait until the train has almost come out of the tunnel, if you know what we mean. Digging a hole can take several minutes, which will seem very long when you are already clenching your buttocks...

Basic Technique With a Bag

POO→WIPE→PACK IT OUT

After finding a hidden spot, calmly do your deed.

Put your discharge in a small bag.

Find the nearest dust bin and get rid of your bag. Ideally you will have found the dust bin before using this technique. You don't want to carry your bag with you for the next two-and-a-half hours.

Confucius' Poo in the Woods Wisdom

- A sage knows where to go even when the need is not yet there.

- Walk like a mouse, dig like a mole, relieve yourself like an elephant, then leave like a snow leopard.

- The man who sees too small or anticipates too little will go to sleep with a smelly hand.

- Silence is a true friend who never betrays.

- The man who blows loudly will attract the curious.

- If a man follows a straight line when leaving his path, he will quickly arrive at his destination and rarely get lost when returning. If he runs around like a hurried rabbit, he will run to his demise.

- In the night, only a fool will leave with his torch. A sage will open his eyes wide and let nature guide him.

- It is by lifting pebbles first that a man will dig a big hole. It is with tree trunks and rocks that he can cover up an abyss.

- When a man must relieve himself, show him how to do it in nature, rather than teaching him how to build toilets.

- Haste will turn a great enterprise into a great disaster.

A Golden Rule of Camping

When camping in a group, establish right at the beginning the Indian rule of propriety: all members of the group touch food with their right hand only. The left hand will be considered impure as because it is to be used exclusively to wipe bottoms when pooing in the woods.

Go green when you poo

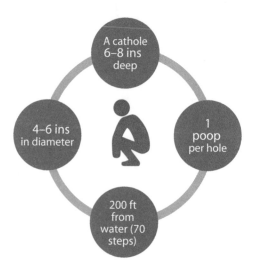

A cathole 6–8 ins deep

4–6 ins in diameter

1 poop per hole

200 ft from water (70 steps)

Help Nature Recycle Your Poo Faster!

When you are in the woods, digging a hole each time for your pooping needs is an important and appropriate gesture you can make for the environment. You can even take this a step further: to accelerate the decomposing of your poo, use the Eco Poo Turbine™. Add some soil, mix it with your poo, and thus help nature "digest" your poo even faster. The soil you use should be as rich as possible (dry dust or sand won't do any good). To mix, always use a wooden stick and never your poo trowel, or you'll break the golden rule of the poo trowel!

If you ever mix your poo with pebbles or dry and infertile soil, the recycling process will be much slower. This is also one of the reasons why the method sometimes used by lazier hikers – neglecting to dig a hole before pooping, but rather hiding excrement under a large rock – should not be used.

When we all do our part to help nature quickly recycle our poos in the woods, we can save the Earth and protect our woods.

Make some money by starting a Poo in the Woods workshop!

Aren't you sick of your job? Wouldn't you like to switch to a career that is closer to nature and that gives more meaning to your life? We have two suggestions for you. Why don't you start organizing workshops on pooing in the woods? In such workshops you can teach hikers how to take care of the environment when pooing in the woods, or how to dig a hole 6–8 inches deep on inhospitable terrain while bursting at seams with the urge to poo. Go for it! Such workshops also have amazing potential as team-building exercises, which you can market to companies. For example, you can split the co-workers into two opposing teams competing to make the most beautiful log toilet.

However, as is often the case, the best way to become rich is not by giving such workshops, but by making others believe that they will become rich by giving them themselves. You can sell workshops on how to lead Poo in the Woods workshops at £2,899, in which the participants earn an International Diploma to become a Poo in the Woods Certified Trainer. To establish your authority, start an Association of Poo in the Woods Instructors, of which you are president, then create a blog entitled, for example, www.I_am_a_master_at_pooing_in_the_woods. com – and build your business from there.

THE POO TROWEL

Stop trying to over-equip yourself! There is one simple tool you will ever need if you want to poo in the woods in an efficient and environmentally friendly manner: the poo trowel. You can find these trowels everywhere, costing from £5 to over £50. The pricier models are particularly lightweight, discreet and sturdy, made of materials conceived by NASA.

Slogans that manufacturers of such trowels have come up with include:

- Poo in the woods with our shovels that are stronger than diamonds!

- Record-holder Tom H. made 9 poo holes in 53 seconds with our trowel!

- When each second counts, choose our trowel. It digs twice as fast as our competitor's!

- Poo trowel XXX is no simple sh*t-shoveller!

But think about it. Do you **really** need a poo trowel that can go to space, that is harder than diamond and that doesn't enter fusion before 670°C? No, what you need is a shovel that will allow you to efficiently pierce the soil while your intestines are in a painful rage, and that won't give you blisters while doing it. That's it. The rest is marketing; don't let yourself be fooled.

How To Find the Right Size of Trowel For Your Poo Holes

Basic Rule for the Use of a Poo Trowel

Scooper ⟵ ⟶ Pooper

NEVER
come in contact!

4 reasons why it is important to make poo holes

- To avoid other hikers from stumbling upon a zone of poo mines or a used toilet paper war zone. If you have encountered this before, you know it's nasty.

- To make sure your poo is recycled as quickly as nature can digest it.

- To avoid polluting water sources.

- To prevent wild animals from sniffing out the odorous leftovers of your hike.

Five Rules of the Poo Trowel

1. **One per person**
   A poo trowel can never be borrowed or loaned.

2. **Use a poo trowel only for poo holes**
   Some hikers try to pack light. In the name of minimizing their load, they use a poo trowel as a mirror, to open beer bottles, to serve pasta to other hikers at dinner... We don't have to spell out why that's a problem, do we?

3. **Do not pack a poo trowel at the bottom of the backpack**
   It should be attached to the exterior of the backpack and be very easily accessible.
   Otherwise, you risk making a spectacle of yourself when the need to poo comes over you and you frantically try to empty the entire backpack in order to find the trowel, screaming: "Fuck, fuck, fuck where's the fucking poo trowel? Don't just stand there, mates, help me find my trowel!"

4. **Even in an emergency, never ask a friend to get your poo trowel**
   A poo trowel is a personal object, and for the well-being of the group, we each take care of our own. In other words, everyone behaves like a responsible adult.

5. **One never leaves one's poo trowel lying around for everyone to see**
   The sight of a poo trowel can kill someone's appetite, and certainly doesn't bring up nice mental images. It is only polite to put it away as soon as it is no longer needed.

And an additional "fair play" rule:

Do not hide a friend's poo trowel. It is not amusing to watch someone search frantically with clenched buttocks.

Three Tools That Can Help When You Are Not Equipped With a Poo Trowel

If you forget your poo trowel, these tools can substitute for it when you make your hole.

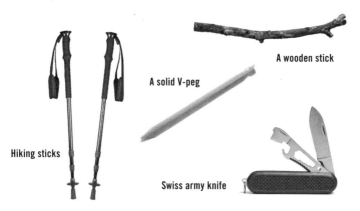

A wooden stick

A solid V-peg

Hiking sticks

Swiss army knife

Tip for camping

When you're camping, don't wait until the last moment. Dig your hole as soon as you pitch your tent. Five days of camping = five holes to dig the first day. Make sure you do not reveal the location of your poo holes to your camping companions. One of them might use one of your holes when in a hurry and not mention it to you, and you will have a stinking situation on your hands that can spoil the mood for everyone. Don't ever randomly accuse someone of doing it, which will pollute the ambiance even further.

Stop Asking For These Items in Outdoor Stores!

The idea of having to poo in the woods unlocks profound fears and provokes very irrational reactions in many people. James P. knows this, because he is subjected to them often. He works in one of the largest outdoor stores in London. In the spring, clients come to his store asking for certain items several times a day. On the following pages, we describe these objects – and remind you that they do not exist. This will save you from making a fool of yourself when shopping for your hiking equipment.

An inflatable toilet

Salesman James P. says:

As soon as people think of holidays, they think of inflatable things: inflatable mattresses, inflatable crocodiles, inflatable dolphins... Inevitably, the idea of buying an inflatable toilet for their holiday soon crosses their minds as well. I am asked at least six times per day about them, sometimes for outdoor use and sometimes for their tents. It's ridiculous – if they just took a minute to think about it, they would realize it's an inane idea. How will you empty it when you have to deflate it? Who will do it? Who will put their mouth to the valve when it needs to be inflated for the second time? Where should the valve be, in the first place? How many people will trip on it and make the contents fall out? Heavier blokes would probably make the thing explode if they sat on it! In short: the demand is there, but for now the technology isn't. From what I could see during initial product testing, we are far indeed from a proper inflatable toilet.

An elastic strap

Salesman James P. says:

It took me a while to understand this one, but having heard it so many times I think I got it. Apparently some people like to read when they go to the toilet. They would like to do that in the forest as well, enjoying the peace and quiet at the same time. Such a poo strap does not exist. Some people insist, and to them I usually sell a car strap that can resist 6.5 tonnes before breaking (I recommend this one because I know that some push with Herculean force...). For additional comfort, some clients then also buy a small pillow to put behind their back at the trendy home décor store next door. I heard from one of our salesmen that one in two slacklines are bought to be used as poo straps, which explains the enormous popularity of this product. I still find that hard to believe...

A strap for two poopers

Salesman James P. says:

Two types of clients ask me about this. Either very young couples still very much in love who want to share everything when they go camping in the woods: the tent, the meal, the mattress — and, of course, their toilet trips as well. Or very close friends who have been going on outdoor trips for years, which synchronized their poo schedules. Both types of clients are looking for a solution that would allow them to share these intimate moments in a more pleasurable way. Again, the product they are looking for does not exist, but when they insist, I sell them a car roof strap as well, this time with a resistance of 13 tonnes — we wouldn't want it breaking. I have to tell them, however, that the 30-day satisfied or refunded guarantee does not apply should they use the strap for pooping purposes. Nobody in our Customer Service department would want to touch it...

PROMOTION: 1,500 POO BAGS FOR £19.99

Salesman James P. says:

This question usually comes from people who own dogs. With all the pooches' poo that they collect in dog poo baggies, they naturally get the idea that they could do the same with their own poo when outdoors. What's interesting is there is usually a discrepancy between the length of their stay and the number of bags they ask for. They'll say something like: "I will be hiking in the woods for a week, so I need a pack of 350 bags." It's automatic. It must be because they are a bit panicked by the idea. I have them do a simple division: 350 divided by 7. They quickly realize that at this rate they would use 50 bags per day, which may be somewhat extreme. I advise my regular clients to buy doggie poo bags instead – they work just as well, they can hold identical volume, they are resistant and waterproof. Also, they are four times cheaper than human poo bags made by some bigger labels who have found a way to capitalize on this problem. And I get asked sometimes by girls if we carry small bags in pink fabric, maybe even embroidered, in which they could hide the doggie poo bag. Some people just have too much money and don't know what to do with it, I swear!

Salesman James P. says:

I haven't figured out yet what the purpose of this would be, but I get asked about this quite often...

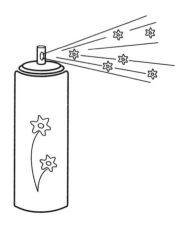

Salesman James P. says:

People, get real! What is the point in removing odours with a perfume called Pine Trees when you are surrounded by actual pine trees? And by the way, if you find yourself in a forest where there are mainly oak trees, and empty a can of Pine Trees after your deed, don't you think that other hikers will smell something fishy there? And just what do you say to people who go hiking in the woods of Wales or Yorkshire and spray the air with lavender-scented odour remover?

Salesman James P. says:

This question comes from people who love to go to remote corners in nature, but who so dislike having to poo in the woods that they don't go on outdoor trips at all anymore. They want to have their own proper portable toilet to place near their campsite. I have to ask these people if they have ever seen any other vacationers bringing their own toilet with them on the roof of their car or in a trailer? They quickly realize that the omnipresence of smartphones would mean they find themselves on top of a Reddit list or get their picture shared all over the world on Facebook or Twitter if they pulled this off. Technically, it is doable, but I doubt anyone would dare bring it on the road.

U.S. ARMY POO SHOVEL

Salesman James P. says:

This question usually comes from clients who have already bought one of those tiny shovels that have recently appeared on the market, intended for making poo holes. But these shovels have had many issues. It takes about four minutes to make a hole deep enough, and they usually break before that. People therefore want a solid and reliable shovel that won't let them down. They usually want to know what the US military does or what UK Special Forces use. Our store policy strictly prevents us from any association whatsoever with war, so I can't help them. I know that many will find a solution themselves; maybe go hiking with a massive shovel attached to their backpack. Others tell me that they will call the army themselves. I don't know what comes out of that...

Warning
Man at
work
in the woods

Salesman James P. says:

Clients who have had the unfortunate experience of being stumbled upon by other hikers when pooping in the woods are eager to find this product. They imagine it as a portable warning sign in a flashy yellow colour that they could put near the spot where they want to relieve themselves. That way they could warn other hikers that someone has ventured off the path and is trying to poo in peace where they are walking. Doubtless such a sign would be handy, but sadly it doesn't exist (yet). And in practical terms: do you think anyone would really want to carry it with them all day, in plain sight of other hikers?

SMELLY POOP DO NOT CROSS

Salesman James P. says:

My clients ask me about biodegradable yellow warning tape printed with the words: "Smelly Poop – Do Not Cross". They plan to use it to mark the area where they relieved themselves. These are hikers who don't believe in digging holes and burying their poo. They imagine that biologists have developed the kind of tape that will harmlessly decompose at the same rate as the faeces.

With all the articles circulating on the web about scientists doing research on ridiculous things, I have the impression that people don't really know any longer what kind of work scientists actually do.

A poo whistle

Salesman James P. says:

There are two different inquiries about whistles. The first comes from hikers who have been attacked by a wild animal while pooing in the woods. They are still suffering from considerable psychological consequences, and are hoping to find a poo whistle that sounds at a high frequency audible only to animals, in order to scare them away without attracting the attention of other hikers. I am always sad to tell them that such a product doesn't exist.

The other inquiry for a whistle comes from hikers who want a signalling whistle. These are often former scouts. They ask me if I know whether such a whistle exists, and if it comes with a sound code system – for example, three short whistles to tell other hikers that they shouldn't stray from the path because someone is pooping nearby. Honestly, people have an incredible imagination when it comes to finding solutions to problems that come with pooping in the woods.

A poo poncho

Salesman James P. says:

This one is easy to understand. People are looking for a sort of a cape that would let them hide from other hikers the fact that they are pooping in the woods. Such a product has interesting advantages. It briefly captures the odour, and keeps a hiker from having to run far from the camp ground to relieve himself unobserved. It allows you to stay close to the fire with the others when it's cold outside. I also suspect that certain clients want one in order to be able to poo near one another – with friends or their partner, for example – so that they could kill time by chatting while pooping.

The poo poncho doesn't exist as such, but we have dozens of different rain ponchos at the store. I help clients choose the right one by trying it on. They put on the poncho and then squat to check the coverage. They are nicely covered from neck down, which means that the rain poncho will also work as a poo poncho. Some clients even get completely naked before trying it on. I don't ask questions. But I do warn them that in the summer under the sun and in temperatures of 30° this might not be the ideal solution.

A QUESTION OF ANGLES

Many difficulties encountered by hikers wishing to poo in the woods arise from the simple fact that they chose the wrong position, or rather the wrong angle. It is absolutely imperative that you know the right one.

The ¾ standing position

This position is used by hikers overcome suddenly by an extremely pressing urge to poo. They don't have time to find a spot at a sufficient distance to be perfectly sure nobody will walk on them. Such people will adopt the ¾ standing position. This allows them to pull their clothes back on fast enough if another hiker comes across them. Anatomically speaking, all proctologists will tell you that this is a very bad position. It knots the intestine and makes it very difficult for you to expunge your discharge. The evacuation period is multiplied anywhere from 2 to 6 times, which increases the chances of an accidental encounter. The ¾ standing position is not effective at all and you should never, ever use it.

110 DEGREES

This is a position adopted by hikers who have some experience but very poor knowledge of anatomy. They attempt to recreate outdoors the technique they use every day in the comfort of their home. As you have probably already worked out, there is one fundamental problem with the position: it lacks a toilet!

These hikers are putting themselves into a very uncomfortable position, which puts the intestine at a bad angle. Besides not being able to relieve themselves efficiently, such hikers will never experience the pleasure of a peaceful poo in a beautiful forest.

80 DEGREES

This is the ideal position and the one you should always adopt when pooping in a forest. Lowering the centre of your gravity gives you excellent stability, even on an incline. The intestine is in the ideal natural position; the one that nature and evolution have intended for pooping purposes. This position will ensure that you have a strong, supple and fast discharge. Thanks to the speed of execution, you will have the smallest risk of being walked upon in a vulnerable position. Notice the position of the arms on the diagram: many favour this position because it gives them more stability and a better position of the abdomen. Catholics will even put their hands together and pray that nobody wanders by. Recite one or two prayers if you can manage to focus on two things at once. It doesn't cost anything, and some swear that it works. From our point of view, we doubt that God has time to deal with such minute details of our lives, but who are we to judge?

50 DEGREES

What is the most effective position of your arms while squatting?

The Anthropology Department at MIT has done considerable research on this question, but so far nobody has uncovered which of the three positions preferred by the hikers is the most effective.

Let us desribe all three of them, and you can decide for yourself which one works best for you.

Try putting your arms up

According to our own research, this is an excellent technique because it shortens considerably the reaction time when you suddenly have to jump up. The more flexible among you will even be able to leave in a forward roll.

Try crossing your arms

This position will make you seem calm and assured in the event of a surprise encounter, and make the other hiker feel bad for interrupting. (Tip: Instead of pulling your trousers up, stay where you are and say nothing. The hiker will soon feel uncomfortable and leave quickly.)

Try the dangling arms position

This position will give you better stability, as it will lower the centre of your gravity and prevent you from falling. This is the position to take if you are prone to falling.

Won't I soil my shoes?

During their first attempts at squatting in the forest, beginners often wonder if the squatting position won't make them soil their shoes. So low is the position that it gives the impression your bottom is very close to your shoes, which can make you wonder if the poo won't land in the wrong place. This stress is augmented by the fact that practically every human has stepped in dog poo at one time or another and can attest to the incredible tenacity of it when trying to remove it from the affected shoe – not to mention the odours that come with it.

Nevertheless, despite the perceived risk, we think it's important to poo in confidence. Trust us. We guarantee that everything will be fine. For reassurance and better stability, remember to keep your feet well apart.

Natural safety distance.

Used intelligently, a slight incline will allow for greater stability and limit the possibility of falling backwards. This, in turn, will give you a more pleasurable pooping experience. (Remember, this is the ultimate goal.)

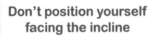

Don't position yourself facing the incline

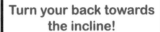

Turn your back towards the incline!

Find the right size bush(es)

Let us remind you that no bush will cover you completely. So you should definitely not choose one that is too small. A bush that hides only your private bits will not be sufficient in the developed world. There are many types of bushes and of course we can't describe all of them here. But fortunately you can ask yourself a simple question: If I were playing hide and seek with my friends, would this bush be a good cover?

Keep your coat and backpack on

Beginners often ask themselves what they should take off when relieving themselves in a forest. Some actually take practically all their clothes off before beginning, especially their shoes and trousers. Perhaps they think that they will be more at ease, or maybe they are keen to recreate as much as possible the primitive nature of pooping in the forest.

This is a mistake. In most cases, we can keep on all the clothes and equipment we are carrying, as it won't get in our way at all. This also allows us to leave the spot in a hurry if necessary.

Attention

Be careful nevertheless: heavy backpacks can cause loss of stability and make us fall on our backs like giant pooping turtles. This is a risk particularly for hikers who have positioned themselves facing an incline. Falling on your back is particularly ridiculous: you will roll down the hill with trousers around your ankles, bum forward. The noise might even attract your friends or other hikers, who will see you butt-naked and stuck on your back. We do not wish this on anyone.

Did you know?

Some hikers take advantage of poo breaks to take beautiful pictures of the surroundings or for close encounters with wild animals that are attracted by the smell.

Diagram 1

Relieving oneself while carrying a backpack

Diagram 2

Taking pictures of nature while doing the deed

Techniques for lateral stabilization in the woods

When squatting, it is important not to fall on the side, to the front, or to the back. Fortunately some tried and tested techniques to prevent that exist. One of them comes from Leonardo da Vinci himself and his Vitruvian man, and another from close observation of tightrope walkers.

The stable duck

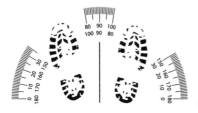

If there is one technique to remember about keeping stable in the forest, it is the duck technique. Once you are in a squatting position, point your feet to the side. Keep your feet apart! This is the only way to achieve stable, quality squatting.

The Vitruvian man technique

Spread your arms as well to help keep you stable. You can eventually lift them a few degrees up or down to see if this helps you with lateral stability.

The farting tightrope walker

Find a small and narrow tree trunk and hold it in your arms. This makes it nearly impossible to fall because we can quickly stabilize as soon as we feel we might fall to the side.

The stabilizing walking stick

Pick a robust and thick stick and trim one end into a sharp tip using your knife. Stick it into the ground in front of the spot you chose to relieve yourself, and knock it deep into the ground with a rock. You can then hold on to this stick for stability.

The stabilizing tree

This technique is identical to the Stabilizing Walking Stick, with the exception that you are holding on to a tree for stability instead of a stick. Follow these tips to make sure you pick the right tree:

Too small

This tree won't hold. You will break it if you fall. This is neither practical nor environmentally friendly.

Good choice

The small diameter of the trunk will allow you to catch yourself in the event of falling.

Too big

A tree of this size has a trunk too large to hold on to. It won't stop you from falling.

The Nordic squat

This is a technique currently gaining momentum at remarkable speed, all due to the increasing popularity of Nordic walking. Vigorous walkers use it for stability, but also for rapidity. It allows you to keep on all your equipment when relieving yourself, and to leave quickly when needed because you don't need to pick up anything before taking off. The sticks can also come handy to fight off smaller animals without interrupting what you are doing.

A double solid

The slogan Better Together is probably what went through the minds of hikers who came up with this technique. Some call it the Eye to Eye Buddy Dump. We actually would not recommend it at all. If nothing else, it obliges you to find a partner with the exact same daily pooping schedule as you. And think of the view!

Techniques on a sloping terrain

Technique #1

Here is a step-by-step guide to pooping on an incline:

1. Find a tree that seems solid and well rooted.

2. Unbutton your trousers with one hand while firmly holding on to the tree with the other. Be careful: this manoeuvre is quite acrobatic and dangerous.

3. Put your feet on each side of the tree and squat without losing your grip on the tree.

4. Relax. Breathe deeply. Relieve yourself.

5. Wipe with whatever you have prepared to that end. (Gather suitable materials beforehand. No respectable *How to Poo in the Woods* reader will go looking for them half-naked after doing the deed.)

6. Pull your trousers back on with one hand and keep holding on to the tree with the other. When done, leave.

Note: Ideally you should make a hole before the above procedure. This is often impossible on inclines, not to mention that a *force majeure* in your intestine could prevent you from achieving it.

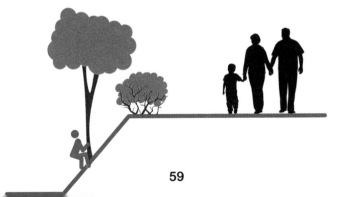

According to our research, the following technique is very popular among climbers. It requires the assistance of a very close friend. If you are by yourself, you could attach your rope to a big rock or a tree trunk. This technique is handy if you want to hide yourself from other hikers when there is no other natural element available for you to hide.

1. Take off your trousers and fold them at the top of the cliff. Attach the harness.

2. Lower yourself a few metres.

3. Check briefly to make sure nobody is underneath you.

4. Lift your legs up and relieve yourself.

5. Wipe yourself with the cord (only if it is not your own).

6. Pull yourself up and put your clothes back on.

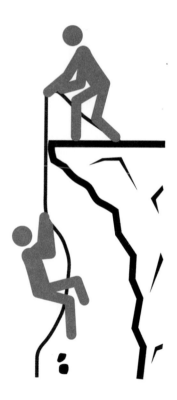

Learn to aim carefully

When you learn to aim with precision, you will know what we call your Anatomical Airdrop Distance. Knowing where exactly the discharge will land will allow you to make smaller poo holes, which will buy you time during preparations. This is not negligible in situations where every second counts!

To discover your distance, find a twig when squatting and make two small lines behind your heels. Once the cargo is unloaded, you will discover your "natural airdrop area". It is anatomically determined and therefore doesn't change from one time to another. That way you will know exactly the spot where you can expect delivery the next time, enabling you to make a smaller hole and gain precious time.

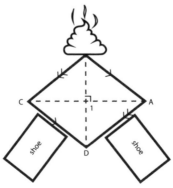

How to use cut tree trunks

Cut tree trunks are tempting because they can be used many ways as a very convenient pooping tool. We present some of them here. However, out of respect for loggers and their working environment, we do not recommend you use them if an alternative is available.

Be careful, this technique is much more difficult than it seems! The risk of falling backwards while in the throes of pooping is extremely high.

The dorsal stabilization of this position allows for complete abandon. No risk of falling backwards.

This technique is less efficient and less practical than dorsal stabilization (opposite).

This is the most efficient way to recreate the position that most closely resembles how you sit on a regular toilet. For more comfort, place some moss under your thighs.

The winning combination of Poo in the Woods techniques

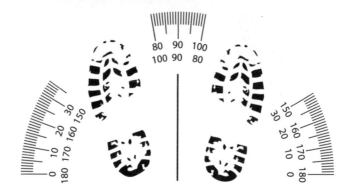

The stable duck

+

Squat on a strong incline

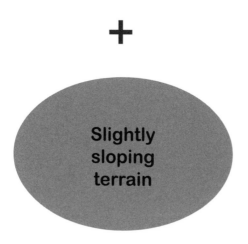

Slightly sloping terrain

WIPING: THE BIG TEST OF NATURAL TECHNIQUES

Wiping techniques are big stress-inducing factors for hikers. In a WWF study published in 2015, 36% of those asked had never pooped in the forest for fear of having to resort to natural techniques for wiping, 58% stated they had no idea what natural techniques for wiping were, and 53% refused categorically to relieve themselves in nature, not even under extreme pressure, if they didn't have at least one big roll of toilet paper in their backpack. Reflected in these numbers is the incredible hold that the toilet paper industry has over the English.

And how did this come to pass? While it was the Chinese who invented toilet paper in the eleventh century, it was the American Joseph Gayetty who launched the industrial production of toilet paper. This was his life's work. It began in 1857 when he spent entire nights conceiving and then constructing industrial machines capable of producing thousands of packages of toilet paper in one day. Then he had to develop a distribution network. To convert Americans to the regular use of toilet paper, he focused his marketing on the medical aspect: "Toilet paper will wipe away your haemorrhoids!". We agree that this was an excellent idea for the time. We should also remember that self-service supermarkets did not exist yet. This meant that a person buying toilet paper had to ask at the counter: "Hello, I would like some toilet paper please!" Which was basically saying: "Hello, I have painful haemorrhoids!" In small towns, rumours spread fast, and you could be certain that in less than a week after buying the toilet paper, the whole village was informed of your problem, and that the more entrepreneurial neighbours would be trying to sell you herbal tinctures to be applied locally.

Thousands of advertisements later, we are now all persuaded that toilet paper is one of those essential objects that we cannot live without. Each person consumes on average at least 24 rolls of toilet paper per year (up to 342 rolls for the bigger consumers, some of whom can be find in the offices of our publishers). Together, the inhabitants of the Western hemisphere unroll several billions of toilet paper rolls in the intimacy of their homes each year.

And yet, humans have done without toilet paper for thousands of years. In some remote corners of the UK, toilet paper was introduced only after the Second World War. Until then they used natural techniques or recycling, and according to historians, they were very happy with them.

When you first experience the incredible efficiency and the gentle freshness and harmony that are the result of using natural wiping resources – and these are not just tree leaves! – you will immediately realize that the preponderance of toilet paper is the result of an international conspiracy spawned in the offices of major toilet paper producers and their clever marketing teams. Their CEOs have formed a secret global alliance. This is how they have been able to impose on 99.99% of the world toilet paper that is inefficient, unreliable and, in terms of overall quality, is far beneath what nature has to offer.

They changed our lives completely in order to make profit. In our opinion, the British should not be in supermarkets on Saturdays, buying up giant packs of toilet paper rolls, but rather in nature with their families, gathering enough plants and pine cones to be able to wipe for a week. It would also be way less embarrassing to run into your boss with a bucket full of flowers and plants than on the Asda parking lot while trying to fit five supersize packs of toilet paper in the boot of your car, because you absolutely wanted to take advantage of the Buy 4, Get 5 promotion. Our ideal society is a world where every family gathers different natural objects according to their preferences. This would be done in a sustainable manner, where everyone would take only as much as they needed. Alas, this is only a dream for now.

THE GOLDEN RULE OF NATURAL WIPES:
Always gather the necessary material before; never after!

Under no circumstances should you wait until the last moment to find in nature something to wipe yourself with. Short-sighted hikers will find themselves shuffling around the forest half-naked, looking like penguins madly searching for something, anything, to wipe themselves with. Never try to take shortcuts with the golden rule of natural wiping. Even when you are about to explode, you must take the time to gather enough wiping material before unleashing the accumulated pressure on your intestines.

THE NATURE CONSERVATION AND SUSTAINABLE LIVING RULE:
Never take more than what you need.

We mention this rule because it is quite common for hikers to over-equip themselves in a panic. They break an entire bush, pull out 50–70 ferns or break off a two-metre branch of a pine tree. Be reasonable; learn to know your actual needs and don't take from nature more than what you would actually use.

Proctologist Dr Watson says:

When looking for something to wipe with, hikers usually first think of leaves, as they most resemble toilet paper. After having tested pretty much anything that I could get my hands on in a forest, I can confirm with certainty that leaves are the least efficient natural wiping tool. If we are going to use them, we should first take time to examine them and choose ones most appropriate for wiping: leaves that aren't too small and which don't have too many holes. However, applied locally, certain plants have excellent curative and calming properties. Coincidentally, I wrote a 700-page book on the subject, entitled: *76 Essential Plants For Curing Problems with the Anus*. For the moment, I am still looking for a publisher. I have contacted several, but according to them, "the market is not ready for it yet".

Evaluation

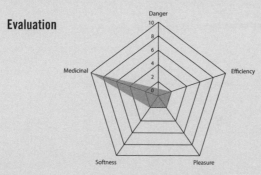

WIPING WITH SNOW

Proctologist Dr Watson says:

Snow is an excellent natural wiping tool that I keep suggesting to my patients during winter. In any case, during the winter there is not much else at hand in nature. Snow is therefore a bit like the pharmaceutical industry selling you tubes of water with the direction: to be used for washing.

Depending on the texture of the snow (powdery, wet...) you may need to let it melt a bit in your hands before applying locally. Snow is beneficial because it tightens the veins locally, which has an excellent calming and cooling effect on your anus.

Evaluation

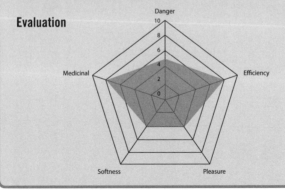

WIPING WITH PINE CONES

 Proctologist Dr Watson says:

A fabulous natural wiping tool – you would think Mother Nature created it exactly for that purpose!

A pine cone should be used gently in the direction of growth of scales, and against the growth of scales for an excellent scrubbing effect. The latter can be painful for those with sensitive bum holes. Watch out also for freshly fallen pine nuts that are still seeping sap – using those could lead to a problem that we professionals call the sticky bum crack. It causes problems because you cannot walk normally for several hours afterwards, and requires local application of a lubricant or other ointments to re-establish the natural rubbing of buttocks.

Evaluation

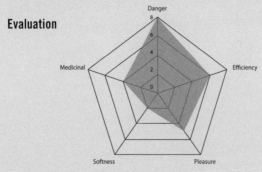

Proctologist Dr Watson says:

You can hope that the forest you are walking in was once under water, and that the rocks and stones you will find are nicely smooth and rounded. Otherwise this technique will be painful with the risk of deep cuts. Use this tool only when there is nothing else at hand.

Evaluation

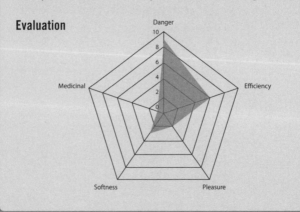

Proctologist Dr Watson says:

It probably goes without saying that if you find a nice patch of soft and cool green moss, you should definitely use it. The results are astonishing. All the marketing people who promise extra softness for toilet paper can just pack up and go home: no toilet paper will ever procure sensations that are even close to what moss can do for you. I sometimes wipe with it just like that, even if I hadn't pooped beforehand.

Evaluation

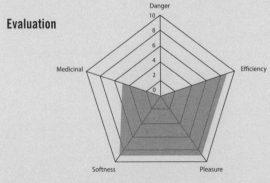

WIPING WITH DIY CHŪGI

Proctologist Dr Watson says:

Many centuries ago, certain Chinese and Japanese used special spatulas. I am a medical doctor and not a historian, so those who would like to know more about them should start by reading the Wikipedia page on "sh*t sticks", followed by the articles it references. I've never tried these chūgi, but it seems to me that it's not exactly Japanese cutting-edge technology. If you have a Swiss knife, you won't need to be MacGyver to make a dozen of them for this millennial experience.

Evaluation

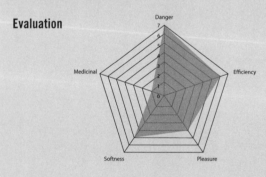

WIPING WITH PINE NEEDLES

Proctologist Dr Watson says:

I thought of this technique when I was on vacation in the South of France. I positioned myself at the top of a rocky inlet, with a splendid view of the Mediterranean. This is the best memory I have of this vacation. Pine needles are very effective. Be careful to use them in the direction of needle growth – my wife tried it the other way around and, according to her, it hurts like bejesus.

Evaluation

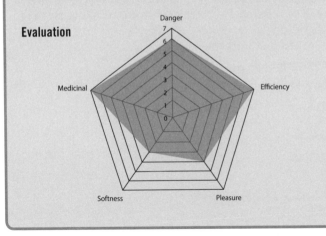

Proctologist Dr Watson says:

This is a technique I invented myself. I had the idea in Japan while using their fabulous toilets that have water jets to rinse your bum. This technique uses a sports water bottle to spray a powerful spurt of water. I like to put a few sprigs of rosemary and lavender in the bottle a few days ahead of my hike to create a rinse that I call A Beautiful Day in Provence. A friend of mine once took a whole bottle of lemon juice instead of water, claiming it had excellent antiseptic properties. That may be true, but I once heard him screaming from the bushes. He didn't say anything when he came back, and I never saw him with a bottle of lemon juice again.

Evaluation

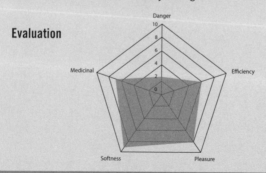

OUR SOLUTIONS TO THE MOST COMMON PROBLEMS ENCOUNTERED WHEN POOPING IN THE WOODS

In this section you can read and learn how to deal with a large number of potentially embarrassing situations that can occur when you poo in the woods without careful consideration. Don't get caught short!

DESPERATE URGE TO GO WHEN YOU'RE IN A GROUP

Situation:

You are on a group hike when the urge to poo completely overtakes you. You are not friendly enough with your fellow hikers to announce: "Guys, I have to take a dump right this minute. Wait for me, will you?" What's more, if you did, you'd be giving yourself an added pressure: you would find yourself worrying that your buddies were debating how it is taking you an unusually long time, what you could possibly be doing, whether you are sick... You know how it goes.

SOLUTION

1. Distancing yourself from the group is never a good idea. Someone will notice, and a search party will find you squatting half-naked.

2. It is important to show that you are driven by altruism – doing your utmost for the group and very little for yourself. Look at the map and say: "The rest of this trail looks tricky. Let me go and check things out!"

3. Run! (Important: never reveal your true feelings. Do not hold your bum, or your belly.)

4. Once you are at a sufficient distance, poo as appropriate.

5. Return to group and say: "It's like I thought, we should keep left/right." Obviously, you haven't checked the path at all.

Expert Opinion

After dozens of tests, I still haven't concluded which technique is better in such situations: running towards the toilet or poo spot, which gains you time, but only makes the situation worse, or walking calmly and slowly, which takes a lot of precious time.

Testimonial

I made friends with a really nice girl in the group. The problem was that each time I tried to distance myself from the group, she said she'd come with me. The fourth time this happened, I was at the end of my wits and couldn't take it anymore, so I yelled at her: "Leave me alone, you stupid bitch, can't you see I have to shit in the worst way??" After that she never spoke to me again, and neither did the rest of the group. I haven't been invited on a group hike ever since. *Terrence, 33*

WILD ANIMALS ARE OBSERVING YOU AND YOU CAN'T DO IT

Situation:

You are trying to poo in the woods, but you can't do it because all the animals are looking at you. Sometimes they really are looking at you, and sometimes you will just feel believe that you are being observed by a rabbit, birds, a bear or a herd of deer. This is a pervasive and irrational fear that scientists call zookickbackphobia.

SOLUTION

1. Neuro-linguistic programming can develop behaviour that will enable you to poo in the forest. By using all your senses, you will make your brain believe that you are in a safe environment – and not in a forest where menacing rabbits are looking at you with their mean little eyes.

2. Once you are in a squatting position, close your eyes and relax by taking deep breaths. Now think of your own toilet – and nothing else.

3. Activate all your senses: think of the coolness of the toilet seat when you sit down, the smell of your toilet freshener, the texture of extra-thick toilet paper gliding over your skin...

4. These positive thoughts will activate the same areas of your brain that are used when you are comfortably sitting on your own toilet. They will relax you and allow you to let yourself go.

Expert Opinion

I know this problem well. I have created an MP3 album entitled Forrest Poo NLP relaxation®. You can buy it for £9.99 and keep it on your smartphone. When you are in position, start listening: I will speak to you in a deep voice, calm and hypnotizing, and help you through all the stages of pooing in the woods. I have received very positive feedback!

Testimonial

I seem to attract only psychos. My last boyfriend took pleasure in having animals observe him while he pooped. He plastered the walls of his toilet with images of does, deer and rabbits. It took me two years to understand why. *Veronica, 32*

YOU USED A POISONOUS LEAF TO WIPE YOURSELF AND YOU ARE TEMPORARILY PARALYZED

Situation:

You are hiking through a tropical forest, full of unfamiliar vegetation. You picked the wrong leaf to wipe your bum with. It looked nice and silky, but it was a trap set by Mother Nature herself: but as soon as you finish wiping, you stiffen. You are completely paralyzed and lying half-naked next to the hole that you just filled.

The solution is also appropriate in a case of snake bite in the wrong spot.

arrrrghhh

SOLUTION

1. There is no way around it: you will need help. However, don't cry out. Otherwise, your companions will gather around and discuss what to do while you're lying there with your trousers around your ankles.

2. Call only your closest friend in the group, without mentioning why. ("Paul, can you come here, please?")

3. When he arrives, slowly and clearly explain what happened. Then ask him to use his water flask to rinse the area with a squirt of water.

4. If this doesn't help, you will have to destroy the proteins of the poison with heat. Ask your friend to use a lit cigarette or a burning stick and bring it as close to the affected area as possible – without burning.

5. This should help. If he is the kind of friend who first took photos to taunt you with in the future, take time to negotiate and make him delete them.

Expert Opinion

Thailand had such a high rate of incidents that illustrated information boards were erected at the entrance of each natural park with warnings: "Mortal danger: Do not wipe yourself with the following plants." Rangers are also trained to warn visitors of dangerous plants in nine languages. As far as I know, Thailand is the only country to take such measures.

Testimonial

I wasn't paralyzed, but it wasn't good: my anus quadrupled in size. It was pure hell to explain why I needed immediate repatriation in a lying (not sitting!) position to my insurance company – first to its call centre operator and then to two of her perplexed supervisors. *Carl, 23*

A PRETTY GIRL/HANDSOME BLOKE COMES RIDING BY ON A HORSE

Situation:

The problem with horseback riders is that they come very fast and appear out of nowhere. This makes it more likely that you will be stumbled upon by a horseback rider than a hiker while you poop: you can usually hear the latter soon enough to be able to get up and dress before he sees you.

SOLUTION

1. As the rider approaches, you have less than one second to get in the position of Apollo, Tarzan, an Amazon or a nymph.

2. Riders are human beings, which is why they often have fantasies of having sex in the wilderness with an unknown beautiful native.

3. Seeing you half naked in the beautiful wild setting could set them off and make for a wonderful opportunity for hot spontaneous sex with a stranger in the wild.

4. If it doesn't, it's still better they come upon you in this position than the squatting one. You can't lose anything by trying.

Expert Opinion

I ride horses. Above is a technique that I invented. I use it when I am in such a hurry that I don't have the time to tie my horse to a tree.

Testimonial

I saw a group of children on a Follow the Traces of Wildlife educational walk gather around the spot where I had pooped an hour earlier. I heard the guide ask the group: "So, children, what do you think: is this a horse poo or a deer poo?" I had the answer to that question, and it wasn't a horse or a deer... *Paul, 46*

YOU HAVE TO RELIEVE YOURSELF ON A SAFARI, DESPITE THE PRESENCE OF DANGEROUS ANIMALS

Situation:

After several hours in the four-wheel vehicle admiring all the dangerous wildlife, you are taken by a strong urge to poo. You will have to find a way to relieve yourself, because you are a long way from base camp.

SOLUTION

1. Explain your situation to the other participants of the safari and refuse all the solutions they offer (squatting on the car bench aiming for a water bottle cut in half, pooping out of the window while the driver honks and squirts windscreen liquid to scare the animals...)

2. Exit the car on the opposite side of the wild animal. The vehicle will serve as a shield.

3. Squat and do your deed.

4. If an animal starts moving, the car should move with it in order to protect you. You should follow the car as well by making crab-like movements to stay out of the animal's eye sight. (Do not make any sudden movements!)

5. As for wiping off, don't take any unnecessary risks, and ask the driver to spill some water on your bum from his jerry can.

Expert Opinion

With thousands of visitors every year, Kenyan safari agencies worked together to find a solution: they installed handmade half-open toilets on the vehicle roofs. Clients climb up through the window. Out of sight of other passengers and the animals, they have an uninterrupted view of the savannah. Many climb back inside with a big smile on their face.

Testimonial

The driver had his eyes on me instead of the zebra. Not surprisingly, 30 seconds into it I was fighting off a zebra with my trousers around my ankles! *Valerie, 46*

YOU NEED TO GO IN THE WOODS DURING THE NIGHT

Situation:

You are camping in the middle of a forest that is as wild as it is beautiful. In the middle of the night you suddenly feel the urge to poo. You will have to go out into the dark unknowns of the forest. The idea of it wakes up your irrational childhood fears.

SOLUTION

1. When we need to poo in the middle of the night, none of us want to go out into the cold, dark night. We tell ourselves that if we go back to sleep, the urge will go. It won't. Pooing is a physiological need.

2. Respect the rule: "I feel an urge. I must act immediately. I will go out of the tent to relieve myself."

3. Put on your head torch. Walk 20–30 metres away from the tent in a straight line.

4. Squat and turn off your head torch – you don't want to attract a cloud of insects, which happily bite you the exposed parts of your body.

5. Forge that you are alone in the woods at night by admiring the stars.

6. Try to enjoy it. You have the universe just for you!

7. Return to the tent.

Expert Opinion

To find the tent on the way back, attach reflective material on it when you pitch it. Another solution: poo in front of your neighbour's tent and get up early to tell everyone that your neighbour has again pooped in the middle of the campground and should be expelled from the group.

Testimonial

I was in one of the US wilderness parks with my new boyfriend. I didn't want him to hear me, so I walked far away from the tent. I got completely lost. I had to wait for daylight by myself, lying under a tree. A ranger's dog found me. Such situations occur often in US parks, apparently *Jessica, 28*

YOU ARE IN A SAVANNAH WHEN A LION APPEARS

Situation:

You are relieving yourself behind a grove when a lion appears and starts approaching you dangerously. He does not seem to understand what you are doing and growls menacingly.

SOLUTION

1. Swiftly take off your belt and arm yourself with a stick (a *big* stick).

2. Stand up, puff up your chest and beat it with your fists in order to make it clear to him that you are the dominant species – never mind that your pants are around your ankles.

3. Indicate to the lion with the help of your stick that he should in fact jump to the other side of the grove.

4. If he doesn't obey, smack your belt like a circus animal trainer would.

5. Once the lion is on the other side of the grove, make giant leaps towards your Jeep (run penguin-style and don't waste time pulling up your trousers).

Expert Opinion

Don't try the Irritated Skunk technique in this situation – which, of course, is the technique of projecting a nauseating odour in the enemy's face. It does not work with lions (or rhinos).

Testimonial

I must be emanating a particular odour because not a minute has passed when a giraffe, two gnus, an elephant and three rhinos came to see what animal could produce such a smell. *Giles, 28*

A RANGER FOUND YOUR POO IN THE NATIONAL PARK

Situation:

You used our technique. You distanced yourself from the group to relieve yourself unnoticed. But there is a problem: a ranger stepped into your deed and is now advancing towards the group, looking angry.

SOLUTION

1. Gather your face into a shocked and outraged expression while listening to the ranger complain that someone pooped in the botanical garden where all the endemic species of the park grow.

2. Listen to the ranger explain how and why we should respect the endemic species (you might learn something).

3. When he has finished, turn to face the group.

4. Tell them: "The ranger is right; I find this outrageous as well!"

5. Finish by saying: "How the person who did this will be able to look at himself in the mirror, I don't know. Gerry, I wish you luck."

Expert Opinion

"Bury it or pack it out!" This is how you save the planet, but it also prevents you from getting caught!

Testimonial

The ranger was a national specialist in tracking wild animals. He sniffed my deed for a few seconds and immediately turned towards me. The result: a $1500 fine for "Doing the deed in a protected zone category A++." *Alan, 42*

IT IS VERY COLD AND THE GROUND IS COVERED IN SNOW

Situation:

You are in the mountains during the winter or on the North Pole when the need to poo takes over you. If you uncover your buttocks, they could freeze instantly. You must find a solution.

SOLUTION

1. Don't panic. There is an old and proven Soviet method for such situations.

2. Bring out your gas stove.

3. Set it to 1 (the minimum) and place it on the snow.

4. Take off your pants and squat just enough to be able to hover above the gas stove.

5. Do your deed (warning: don't dump it on the flame; aim right next to it).

6. Get dressed quickly, because in a matter of minutes, dozens of seals or reindeer might start gathering around you, attracted by the minerals that you have just let out.

Expert Opinion

It would not be appropriate to disturb the pristine whiteness of the North Pole or the mountains. Your deed will be deeply frozen in less than 30 minutes under a bit of snow, but nature will not be able to recycle it. The best is to pack it out. Use the method described in this book to do that. FYI, I bought myself a mountain pant with a big butt zip. It turns me into a mountain poo superhero each time I use it.

Testimonial

My boyfriend approached me right after. He didn't know what I had just done. He said: "It's astonishing; it smells like grilled pig here!" I guess I approached the flame a bit too much with my bum and burned off a few hairs... *Laura, 28, telecoms, Birmingham*

YOU WIPED YOURSELF WITH AN UNKNOWN PLANT, AND NOW IT BURNS

Situation:

During a holiday in a foreign country you thought it would be nice to try a new leaf for wiping. Unfortunately, you have chosen a plant species known in this country as a powerful irritant. It was a painful experience. You can't walk. You fear what is to follow the next day.

SOLUTION

1. As soon as you start feeling the pain, walk away penguin-style and look for moss. Don't squirm while walking, or you'll alert others to your problem.

2. Moisten the moss with water from your water flask.

3. Scrub the affected area vigorously in order to remove the irritant as much as you can.

4. Repeat as often as necessary. (However, be careful not to run out of water too soon.)

5. Finish off with a massive and powerful rinse.

6. If you have any milk handy, use it for a final rinse. It will calm the pain, especially if you chose a plant that was actually hot pepper.

Expert Opinion

If milk isn't available, take a wooden stick, put it in your mouth and bite it hard.

Testimonial

I tried to cool the area off with the only thing I had available: a mint perfume called "Polar Fresh". It contains alcohol and mint, and it ended up burning twice as much! *Jay, 42, salesman, Bath*

HOW TO POO IN THE WOODS WHEN THERE IS NO WOOD

Situation:

You have been trekking through a bare desert for several days. No brush or shrub on the horizon; nothing, everything is completely flat. There's nowhere to hide to be able to do your deed without your group seeing you.

SOLUTION

1. Admit to the group that you have to do your deed.

2. This will surely come as a relief to others who no doubt have the same problem. (Do you really think they are all limping because they are just tired?)

3. Distance yourself from the group by about 100 metres.

4. Place your rucksack on the ground. It will serve as a little courtesy curtain.

5. While the group is waiting for you and pretending they aren't watching, do your deed hidden behind your rucksack.

6. While you're at it, reassure everyone watching you from the corners of their eyes by giving them a thumbs-up and yelling: "All good!"

7. Return to the group when finished.

Expert Opinion

Be careful: in a salt desert, sound travels without losing its intensity. A simple fart, even a discreet one, can be heard for over 900 metres.

Testimonial

When I came back, all other people were scattered about as well, doing their deed. All you could see were backpacks and heads. *Alan, 32*

YOU HAVE TO USE AN ECO-FRIENDLY TOILET

Situation:

To protect the forest you are hiking in, several environmentally friendly toilets have been installed along the trail. You are faced with a biological toilet that you have never used before.

SOLUTION

1. Enter the toilet stall made of wood carried there on a donkey's back.

2. Draw the 100% Fair Trade organic cotton curtain.

3. Lower yourself carefully onto the rough wooden seat, to avoid splinters.

4. Do your business, but try to fart as little as possible (methane is a powerful greenhouse gas).

5. Use dry tree leaves in the same manner as ordinary toilet paper.

6. Once finished, pull the vine to make the rainwater run through the reed-bed and flush the toilet.

7. Rub the stone on the eucalyptus log next to the toilet to deodorize.

8. Disinfect the seat with the lemon slices found in a cup beside the toilet.

Expert Opinion

A client once told me that her husband refuses to relieve himself in the forest or such biological toilets. He holds it in and saves it to stink up their toilet at home. He takes a strange pleasure in watching other family members run away holding their noses.

Testimonial

Nobody knew how to use this f***g eco-friendly toilet, which made it stink really badly. Everyone went to the toilet with their spray can of air freshener, thereby contributing heavily to the hole in the ozone layer! I'm not sure if the carbon balance of such toilets is really positive. *Oliver, 24, courier, Luton*

DEALING WITH WILD ANIMAL ATTACKS IN THE WOODS

Did you know...
a deer can hear a fart 7.3 km away?

If the winds is favourable, he can even sense a human flatulence from over 13 km away. The olfactory and auditive capacities of deer are quite simply astonishing.

There is no technique that can guarantee you perfect safety while pooping in the forest. However, a good knowledge of animal behaviour can significantly reduce the number of attacks. Knowing Poo Self Defence® techniques will prevent you from being abused while half-naked on the ground by an animal angered by your presence on its territory.

For decades, hikers believed that the only thing they could count on was the sheer unpredictability of wild animal attacks. Ethologists disagree with this completely. "Animals have perfectly good reasons for attacking us in such situations. It is only our lack of understanding of their behaviour that makes us think they are random and unpredictable," says Tom Paktinso, a Canadian ethologist. He has been studying wild animal attacks on hikers for 18 years, so he should know.

WHY DO WE HAVE SO MANY DIFFICULT ENCOUNTERS WITH ANIMALS?

The explanation is readily understandable even by novice ethologists. The attacks are connected to the incredible olfactory capacities of animals. It is quite easy to understand. Even humans are quite sensitive to and bothered by the odour of farts and poop of other humans. We find these odours very strong. When you relieve yourself in a forest, just imagine how would an animal feel whose sense of smell is a hundred times more developed then yours. For many animals this is olfactory torture. They often approach you by curiosity at first, to see which animal can possibly smell this way. Some of them will then try to stop the torture by attempting to eliminate the one emitting it.

As a result of evolution, we share a big portion of our genome with animals. They are attracted by primitive sexual scents that we produce when defecating. Biologists will tell you that we confuse many attacks with something else. The "attackers" are often males in rut who are attempting to seduce and reproduce. The press has recently published disturbing stories about this – you have probably come across them as they have been widely shared on social networks, often accompanied by graphic photographs.

Some animals attack forest poopers for a very basic reason: you are shitting in their dining room. Imagine you come home and find it filled with a nauseating smell, only to realize that it is coming from the dining room where a stranger is shitting on your Persian rug. How would you react?

And finally, let us share with you the idea of Tim Smith from the Evolutionary Biology department at the University of Alaska: several animals understand that you are in a vulnerable position without much room for manoeuvre when pooping, which makes you easy prey. Just like wolfs prefer to attack lambs who stray from the herd, wild animals prefer to attack us when we are away from our group and thus at our most vulnerable.

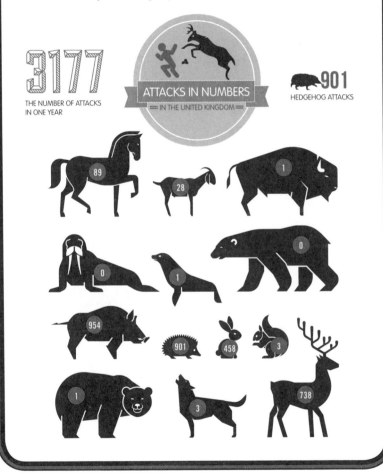

3177
THE NUMBER OF ATTACKS
IN ONE YEAR

ATTACKS IN NUMBERS
=== IN THE UNITED KINGDOM ===

901
HEDGEHOG ATTACKS

The Golden Rule:
Never try a penguin escape!

Whatever the size of the animal that attacks you, the penguin escape will never do any good – it can actually increase the danger you are in because you easily fall. In a panic, always use one of our techniques.

107

A bear confronts you while you are pooing in the woods

This is a more common occurence than you may think.

The bear probably didn't come to attack you; he is just curious to see what you are doing there. Stand up and start waving your arms. You should also talk. As you probably don't know what to tell a bear, take the easiest approach: insult him! (For example: "Ugly bear, go bonk your mother, I bet she is hairy like you!") Don't run away, but rather distance yourself slowly penguin- or crab-style. Don't bend to pull up your trousers, as this will make you look like "the smaller animal" and thus less scary to the bear.

Example 2: The bear charges towards you while you are pooing in the woods.

Don't panic. Almost all bear charges are "bluff charges". Don't run away! Don't forget that the bear can run faster than a competitive sprinter. The trousers you have around your ankles won't help your speed either. Also, seeing you run might unleash the hunter instinct in the bear. Don't climb a tree, unless you can do it incredibly fast and climb high. Instead, slowly get up, wave your arms and talk very loudly.

Example 3: The bear is extremely aggressive

Pretend to be dead. Adopt a foetal position in order to protect your vital organs, don't move and don't make a sound. Surprised bears usually stop attacking once you are no longer a threat (or dead).

Three more tips to avoid being attacked by a bear

1. If you want to limit the risk of being attacked, bring a saucepan and a spoon with you. Make a noise by tapping the saucepan with the spoon while you are relieving yourself.

2. Don't snack while you are pooping, as the smell of food attracts bears.

3. You are allowed to carry a gun for protection in American state parks. If you have a gun, you can also use it as a prop while you poop. Like many rangers, we do not believe that carrying a gun is necessary in a park. In fact, it is more dangerous for you than for a bear.

What to do when attacked by a wild boar

Wild boars have an excellent sense of smell but very poor eyesight. Those who might attack you will usually be young curious boars that are looking for some adrenaline in their young lives. In most cases they will approach you, but they won't attack. Get up, find a stick on the ground and keep the animal at a distance until his mother calls him.

What to do when attacked by two hedgehogs

A female hedgehog comes along with her baby hedgehog while you poop. You panic: the mother will surely surge toward you to protect her little one. Stand up and wave your arms in large circles. The hedgehog will roll up in a ball, which will give you the opportunity to run away.

What to do when attacked by a deer

If you are in a squatting position with your head held low, the deer will come charging at you with his head lowered in order to test if you are the dominant one in this confrontation. Considering you are not exactly in a stable position, you risk falling if this happens. You will be better off if you stand up quickly and raise your arms to show the deer that you are bigger than what he thought. He will be surprised and back away. This will give you a chance to slowly recede with your arms still up. After that the deer will probably be more interested in what you left behind, and let you run to safety.

How to react when attacked by a kangaroo

When the kangaroo jumps out of the bushes, immediately get out, free one of your legs and start kicking him kung-fu style. Continue until there is a clear winner. Good luck!

Discover the safest techniques

Bad technique

Fairly bad technique

The only known technique for pooping safely in the forest

1. Find two trees about 6–9 metres apart. Throw a rope onto the first tree.

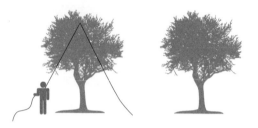

2. Throw a second rope onto the second tree.

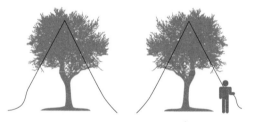

3. Prepare yourself by lowering your trousers and put on a harness. (*Don't* try to use your underpants as a harness.)

4. Call someone you know very well and trust completely. Ask him to pull you up at least 4.5 metres above ground.

5. According to our research, this is a sufficient height so that no animal can catch you (too high for bear claws or a horny deer). Relieve yourself while holding on to the rope. Admire the view above the canopy.

Our tests suggest that at this height, the animals won't even notice you in 93% of cases.

HOW TO MAKE YOUR OWN POO TUBE

Poo tubes were invented by people who want to protect nature by not leaving a single trace behind. The idea behind it is virtually the same as when we collect our dogs' excrements: we collect our own excrement in a poo tube and transport them to a place where we can dispose of it safely and without any harm to the environment.

Poo tubes are particularly useful in areas where the ground is dry, or at high altitudes with low temperatures. Anaerobic soils also slow down considerably the process of decomposition of human faeces. When you are very high in the mountains with permanent snow, or at Earth's poles, what happens to your poo is the same that would happen if you put it in the freezer. It will freeze and decompose extremely slowly.

Avid practitioners of activities such as white-water rafting and other water sports, as well as climbers or hikers, mountaineers and other nature enthusiasts are increasingly carrying on their backs what minutes before they carried inside them. These sportspeople are coming up with increasingly sophisticated techniques of poo elimination to suit their particular needs. Skiers and ski touring enthusiasts are the most advanced because they attach particular importance to the solidity of their poo tubes. They certainly don't want them an explosion in their backpacks after a big fall. Climbers have also had to find a solution as well, since the most popular routes started to smell really badly. (If you would like to learn how to safely poo while hanging on a rope at 600 metres above ground, and to successfully catch your poo in a poo tube, contact your local climbing association and ask about indoor training.)

Contrary to what you might think, using a poo tube is not like using a tiny toilet. You don't aim into the opening and close it immediately after. Just imagine the smell on the seventh day of your hike! Instead, you will use greaseproof paper and Furoshiki, a type of traditional Japanese wrapping cloth traditionally used to transport clothes, gifts, or other goods.

Also, don't go to outdoor stores looking for poo tubes in sizes S, M, L or XL. They don't exist. You will have to make your own with material that can be found in any hardware shop. Prepare to spend at least £20. The effort will all be repaid in the sense of pride you will feel at creating and using a poo tube and the contribution you will be making to the protection of the environment.

Here are three everyday objects that can be used as a poo tube in a pinch. What they have in common is that they are 100% airtight.

A Tupperware box

An airtight jar

122

A PVC Waterproof Dry Bag
(packable boater's dry bag)

MAXIMIZE YOUR SAFETY!

Some hikers will go as far as placing a Tupperware box or jar into the waterproof dry bag for maximum protection. When it comes to poo transportation, you can never be careful enough.

POO TUBE AND FUROSHIKI METHOD

The most efficient technique that we will describe here for you combines an ancestral Japanese tradition and a well-known Mexican dish.

1. Bring along some large sheets of greaseproof paper

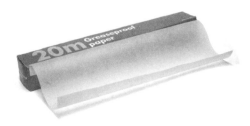

2. Place a sheet on the ground.

3. Poop by aiming at the centre of the sheet. (You can draw targets on the sheets beforehand for fun.)

4. Roll up your poo as if you were preparing a nice warm burrito.

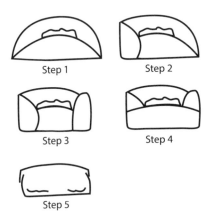

Step 1   Step 2

Step 3   Step 4

Step 5

5. Variation: Use the Japanese Furoshiki technique

6. Secure everything with some scotch tape.

7. Place your burrito or furoshiki in a plastic bag stored previously in your poo tube.

BE CREATIVE: DEVELOP YOUR OWN FOLDING METHOD!

We have shown you two simple folding methods, but the possibilities of poo wrapping are endless! Come up with your own poo folding method and use it as a form of self-expression. However, we strongly advise you against practising any new method in actual conditions. Simulate these at home with an A4 sheet of paper, placing a small quantity of mashed brown beans shaped in the middle, and then try wrapping them using your folding technique. If you have mashed beans on your fingers at the end of your trial, you should most definitely not use this technique in a forest.

HOW TO EMPTY A PACKED POO TUBE?

Don't wait until the end of your three-week hike to empty your poo tube. Do it every time an opportunity presents itself. You can leave the contents of your poo tube in a container in a park, in a dog poo bin, or in a large waste bin.

Be nice: if a kind local invites you for a drink in his home, don't dump your poo in the dustbin or block the toilet by emptying seven days worth of poo in it.

EQUIPMENT YOU WILL NEED BEFORE YOU EMPTY A POO TUBE

If, like many, you are too tired at the end of a long hike and don't put away your gear or wash your clothes for days, be aware that the more you wait, the more painful the emptying of your poo tube will be. If you are lazy, buy a gas mask in a hardware store.

Poo tube left sealed for three weeks

Poo tube left sealed for 1 month (or left out in the sun)

Poo tube left sealed for 1 year or more.

THE HARDENING OF RULES IN NATURAL PARKS

Natural parks attract large numbers of visitors, which is why ever stricter regulations for their use have been imposed. Poo tubes are already obligatory in some natural parks and some popular climbing destinations. In a few years poo tubes will be obligatory in numerous parks. You should therefore not be surprised if rangers want to inspect the contents of your poo tube when you exit the park. They will check whether the contents of your poo tube correspond to the weight in kilos proportional to the number of days spent in the park.

A ranger will probably wait for you in a small cabin at the entrance or exit of the park and weigh your poo tube. He is also authorized to ask you to open the bags inside your poo tube to check whether they are filled with actual poo, thus making sure you didn't cheat by filling them up with soil or mud.

Yes, there will be cheats, who will try to insist that an empty poo tube after a five-day hike can be explained by constipation. We assume that in such cases, two muscly rangers will undertake a painful examination to determine whether such hikers are actually constipated or have emptied their bowels in the park. There might even be X-ray machines installed to check this. We hope that parks won't go that far, but don't forget that the pressures of nature conservation are considerable. We are quite pessimistic about the evolution of regulations in the coming years. We believe in freedom and awareness more than in blind repression.

EVACUATION OF CONTAINERS BY HELICOPTER

Several natural parks are now addressing the issue of human excrements. They have sited toilets or reservoirs where hikers can empty their poo tubes. These reservoirs are airlifted once a year to a treatment facility. Here are the helicopters used and their internal names.

Sikorsky R-6
It can transport up to 360 kg
of poo at maximum speed of 256 km/h

Sikorsky R-52
It can transport up to 970 kg of poo at
maximum speed of 288 km/h

The poo fly

The brown knight

The Kamov K25
It can transport up to 8,230 kg or poo
at maximum speed of 351 km/h

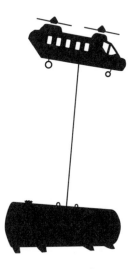

The poo mule

DID YOU KNOW?

If the rope holding these containers were to break and the container explode close to a village, the residents would be doubly cursed. An unbearable smell would force them to evacuate the village for a period of between two and three years. And in the immediate aftermath of the explosion, all the flies from the region would be attracted to the contents, creating a noise greater than that of a plane taking off.

HOW TO MAKE YOUR OWN POO LOG

Our expert Tom Hayatt strongly believes that every hiker or walker should always carry their own poo log. Don't look for one in stores; unfortunately it doesn't exist (yet). Tom Hayatt suggests you buy a notebook and use it for keeping track and to study all your poos in the woods over time. This will benefit you tremendously in your preparations.

Creating your own poo log is quite simple and takes only a few minutes. On top of the basic information like date and time, you can customize it according to your wishes and objectives.

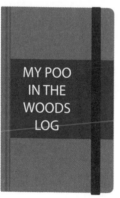

MY POO
IN THE
WOODS
LOG

"Having your own poo log is indispensable if you want to make progress in your poo in the woods techniques."

Tom Hayatt

Tom Hayatt suggests the following poo log categories:
- Incline of the terrain
- Texture/colour/consistency
- Animals in the area
- Other hikers encountered
- Wiping technique employed
- Total time
- Diagram of the zone

EXAMPLE OF A POO LOG

POO IN THE WOODS LOG

LOCATION: St James Park
DATE: Feb 2, 2015
DURATION: 56 seconds
SIZE: Very big!!!
GRADIENTS: 1
DIFFICULTY: 1/5 easy
CONSISTENCY: Pretty soft
WILDLIFE ENCOUNTER: Birdsong
HUMAN ENCOUNTER: Park-keeper
REMARKS: The best part of the visit!

POO IN THE WOODS LOG

LOCATION:
DATE:
DURATION:
SIZE:
GRADIENTS:
DIFFICULTY:
DIARRHEA:
WILDLIFE ENCOUNTER:
HUMAN ENCOUNTER:
REMARKS:

LET'S REMEMBER A BASIC RULE:
We each have our own poo log!

A poo log is not shared, not even with your best friend or spouse — not even in the name of saving money or of lightening the load in your backpack. A poo log is like your personal diary; something that you keep only for yourself.

DID YOU KNOW?

Having a poo log can help you avoid fines in the US and Canada. Since 2011 these have been recognized by American and Canadian authorities as acceptable forms of proof. Internet forums suggest that when accused of defecating in the forest by often humourless rangers, several hikers were able to demonstrate that they had not yet pooped that day by showing them their poo log. So if you go hiking in North America, keep a poo log faithfully!

DON'T GET CAUGHT!

Faced with an increasingly massive influx of visitors to their natural parks and the ecological problems caused by tens of thousands of hikers defecating in their forests, Canada and the United States have come up with a series of rules and interdictions. These are modelled on the programmes of the special forces combating the illegal drug trade, from special badges to the use of heat-sensitive helicopters and sniffer dogs.

REVISE YOUR KNOWLEDGE OF POO IN THE WOODS TECHNIQUES

We've chosen to treat the subject of pooing in the woods in an entertaining but serious manner. As you can see, the issue of pooing in the woods is also a serious ecological issue, especially in natural parks that are particularly popular or when high in the mountains.

In order to revise your knowledge and summarize what you should remember, we recommend that you visit the website of New Zealand's Department of Conservation, or Te Papa Atawhai. Look for the page entitled: "Disposing of human waste where no toilets are provided". There you will find everything you absolutely must know on the subject of pooing in nature on one page.

CONCLUSION

There! You've finished the book. The time passed quickly, didn't it? Thanks to our erudite advice and the sharp opinions of Tom Hayatt, your outdoor activities will never again be spoiled by poo problems. We hope you will now love to poo in the woods.

Now that you have all the knowledge, the techniques described in this book will be a fun topic of conversation during your walks in the woods. You'll see: people will be captivated by your stories. Keep their curiosity piqued by throwing in catchphrases such as:

- Have I told you about the time when I did my deed on a safari and was attacked by a baboon?

- Let me tell you about the time when I was camping and I had to chase half-naked a wild boar who stole my entire stock of toilet paper!

You can go even further: demonstrate the use of a poo trowel or the full process of using a poo tube to your friends. This will really help to create a lively atmosphere – and will surely help to save the planet.

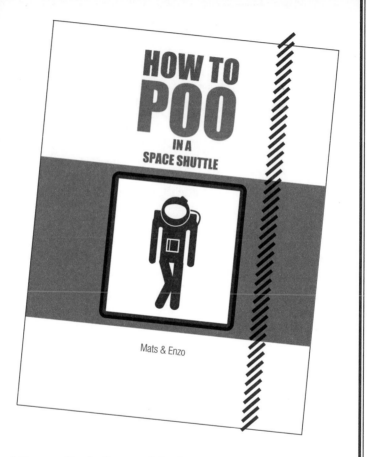

* We are waiting for the green light, data, authorization and testimonials from NASA.

Do you want be an astronaut?
Would you like to travel in space?

Learning how to use toilets in space is an obligatory part of training to become an astronaut or a space tourist. Don't blow a trip that will cost you $15,000,000 because of a toilet issue or space diarrhoea!

In our forthcoming book you will learn:

- How to prepare at home

- How to make your own space toilet simulator in your own garage

- How to train in a public swimming pool without being banned for life

- How to train on earth to be able to catch flying objects in space

- How to ace the selection tests

- How to make the instructors believe that you don't go to the toilet that often, in order to get an advantage over other candidates

- How to pass the the tests for using a toilet mounted on a centrifuge

- How to open a space suit in an emergency in less than 2 hours, 35 minutes

- How to prevent take-off simulations from making you want to go to the toilet each time

- How to prepare psychologically to cope with dramatic poo-related situations that can occur in space

- How to deal with the shock of a flush that doesn't work — and won't work for the rest of the trip

- How to handle with dignity a thundering case of gastroenteritis

- How to cope in the event of aseptic tank of the space ship exploding

- How to explain to your fellow astronauts that you broke the sanitation system

POO IN THE WOODS LOG

LOCATION: _____

DATE: _____

DURATION: _____

SIZE: _____

GRADIENTS: _____

DIFFICULTY: _____

STOOL CONSISTENCY: _____

WILDLIFE ENCOUNTER: _____

HUMAN ENCOUNTER: _____

NOTES: _____

_____

_____

_____

_____

_____

_____

POO IN THE WOODS LOG

LOCATION: _____

DATE: _____

DURATION: _____

SIZE: _____

GRADIENTS: _____

DIFFICULTY: _____

STOOL CONSISTENCY: _____

WILDLIFE ENCOUNTER: _____

HUMAN ENCOUNTER: _____

NOTES: _____

_____

_____

_____

_____

_____

_____

_____

POO IN THE WOODS LOG

LOCATION:

DATE:

DURATION:

SIZE:

GRADIENTS:

DIFFICULTY:

STOOL CONSISTENCY:

WILDLIFE ENCOUNTER:

HUMAN ENCOUNTER:

NOTES: